Double You

DOUBLE

YOU

poems

by

Barry Franklin

Book and cover design: Vladimir Verano, VertVolta Design

Cover image: © Justin Kauffman via Unsplash

ISBN: 978-0-578-92111-2

Published by

Barry Franklin *Seattle, WA*

Author contact: bjfpoems94@gmail.com

For Melinda, Derek, and Colin

Contents

THE SEVENTH SENSE

Take it – take another little piece of my brain now, baby
I could use a break from the daily rigor
Mortis and tenons my aching
Joints are jumping and jostling for
Position me by the sea somewhere in the
Morning becomes eclectic break fast say
Grace and start praying
Mantis man this weighs me down,
Cut me up
Autopsy and turvy me
Myself and eyeballing the
Surf cascading sea salt
In my wounds wound into DNA
Coils spiral slinky down the stairway
To heaven and Jupiter and beyond
The sea waiting for me to
Dance the locomotion and the evolution from
Homo Habilis and
Erect us a Taj Mahallway to
A sacred realm where exists
A scale model of Shangri-La
In a plexiglass case of the best
Years of your life are ahead
Of the class of 1999 was a very good year
Of the Rat or some extinct species with
Poor survival skills while

We humans probe space

Travel, make time unravel, pound gavel

Our evolutionary journey onward, uphill

Climb, reach for the sublime and

The sub-lemon twisting the night

Into day breaks blood ruby brain

An express train

Neither sane nor insane

Cut across the grain of

Sand dabs cosmetic thoughts on

Natural instinct and

The mind rationalizes what the brain dictates

So evolution plateaus.....

Lest we stop and smell the

Stench of mindless existence

You can have common sense

I'll take the uncommon variety

Is the splice of life and past lives re-examined

In a new light in

A place way past tense

My future sense of

The seventh sense

I am coming to

Park Bench

Cosmic rays bombard the Earth
Penetrating our bodies and minds
Most of us prioritize mind over matter
Yet we stumble, remaining blind to
This blitzkrieg of positive energy

Forty or so leaves have fallen near this bench
Dead leaves – by next week they'll be
Raked up or scattered by a leaf-blower
But today a few among them respond to
The light breeze cooling this blood-boil day

The few stand erect, then tumble, scrumble and scramble
Driven by the incoming wind's energy
So the question is: will I respond
Like those few leaves: will I dance?
Or stay parked on the bench?

ICE BOUND

Ice bound

Caught in a feeling
I can't feel
Despair

Caught in a web so strong
I can't move
My center

Caught on my outer reaches
I can't reach
Down

To grab me by my scruff
And yank me
Up

Blood hound
Caught in my own smell
Entailed

Eyes found
Caught on the far horizon
I can't see why

Ice bound
Caught in a deep crevasse
Light prison

Caught on a polar cap
I can only go south
Way down

Way off the map
That's where
I'm found

CHAPTERS

Many years ago there was a map
A "W" on it marked a pot of gold
"Why not an "X"?" I queried
But I couldn't find the answer
Anywhere

The plan seemed well plotted
Pretty clear where things were headed
But there was another factor afoot
Twists, turns, that wanton randomness
Everywhere

One day I noted both sons
Were better than I
At basketball and table-tennis
Something was slipping away
No one cared

'Cept me of course, I
Wondered what else would lapse
And elapse and drift slowly past
As things passed en masse
And fled

What is the prime of life?
Perhaps a prime number
One can number the stages
And phases traversed
En route

Milestones like realizing
Your doctor is younger than you
And is quite possibly fallible
Despite what you were led to believe
Aah, me

Your cronies gather to
Discuss their health issues
No whining, just the realization
At some point, you know
The score

And becoming a grandparent
The grandest state of all
Guarding old photos and memories and
Stubbornly holding on
For dear life

My bucket list is full of holes
There are things I'll never see
In person or even dreamland
Like Mount Kilimanjaro
Up close

You master your dreams
Take control of your inner life
Resolve old issues
Once and for all
For all

I succumb to the inevitable
Enjoying my morning macchiato
I knew I was on the downhill slope
When I subscribed to National
Geographic

All the possibilities that
I missed I miss just knowing
They were once right in here
The golden bowl of ecstasy
In which I did dip

Oh, monsters of delight
Called my name and
Attached an ankle bracelet
To monitor my every idleness
Here on Earth

Double You

Wide-eyed, wakeful, worthy
We were wanderers
We were without woes
We weren't whiny witches,
Wooden warlocks
We whistled while we worked
We won World War I
Wherever we went
We were wave warriors
Without a World-wide Web
We once wove
Wondrous words
We were wealthy, wise
Why worry?
Warm, wistful, wonderful

Wait!
Without warning we woke
"Why" we wondered
What will we worship
Without Double You?

Double You,
We will
Worship one another
Would we were wise we'd

Worship one another
Warmth we'll weave when we
Worship one another
We will
Worship one another
Worship one another
Worship one another

I love you so much
I want to double you

PANDEMIC I

This down time calls for introspection
A time to regret some wrongs
To rectify some indiscretions
And remember things forgotten too long

So many years I spent unwoke
So many people I left behind
Ones I treated too dismissively
Would that I had known to be kind

I was drawn to the especially creative
T'would bang my bell of worthiness
Families and friends went undervalued
I overprized intelligence

Now I search the Net all day
Is he still alive? I want to know
Does she still hum on nature walks?
Does he still have a magic glow?

And how does my first little friend look 'bout now?
Were the braces hiding a perfect smile?
Did her father ever face his demons?
Did she and her mother reconcile?

Did that mudslide of repression bury our town?
That bakery with the great French doughnuts – did it go?
Did the school survive my insurrection?
Did my VW"s tires continue to blow?

Did Howie play basketball at Santa Clara?
Did Lizzie marry her handsome exchange student beau?
Is that Timex watch we put in a teenage time capsule
Still ticking somewhere far below?

But my curiosity is mainly focused on
The last thing you said before we were grownup
I never knew for sure what you meant
When you whispered in my ear, "Wait up"!

I'll Remember You

Before the guy was canonized
Lending his name to the breed
What did they call St. Bernards?

Perhaps my mother knew
What a mind she had!
Her memory was so sharp —
She taught me that if you want to remember something,
Repeat it three times

I remember that part
Because she did not look very happy when I told her she meant either
"Say it once and repeat it twice,"
Or "say it three times"
Not, "repeat it three times"

The part of her instruction I have lost is:
"To yourself" or "aloud."
I have tried it a half-dozen times one way and
Maybe 58,000 the other —
They seem to work equally well

Of course, anything poignant is automatically
Committed to memory:
The spiritual heights, the epiphanies,
The laugh of a child that moved you to tears,

Certain smiles beamed your way,
Significant people, special events,
Beloveds,
The day you lost your virginity

Moments of utter despair,
Petty annoyances we should have long ago forgiven,
Painful and obvious snubs…
All remembered clearly.
And everyone remembers exactly where they were
That fateful day
President John F. Kennedy
First hooked up with
Marilyn Monroe

The three-time rule applies when recording far less evocative data:
Historical dates, mathematical formulae, catechism lessons.
But a certain phenomenon, though easily committed to memory,
Is so important, so critical, so special, so vital that
It is worthy of every possible recording procedure known

I'll be dead for eons
That's a very long time not to forget you
So, I'll now say it three times aloud:
"You, You, You!"

And three times to myself:
"   ,   ,   "
And a seventh time just to be sure:
"You"

I'll remember

Born on the 5ᵗʰ of July

I'm a Red Sox Doodle Dandy
Born on the fifth of July
The whole lie, and
Nothing but the lie
Down beside me
Whisper sweet somethings
In my ear plug the
Hole in my dike
I'm bleeding corpuscles
Sore muscles in
Where wise men fear to
Tread pattern of
Complex flex
Time, bend time, break
Time out!
Give me a rest
Reel me in
Unhook me
Slap me into your creel
And take me home land
Secure me
Lock down
Lock up
Look up in
Your dictionary and

Tell me the meaning
Of life….
Surely there's more to it than
This

The Elephant

I was born on the tenth of March
In the year one thousand nine-hundred
And forty-five
With specific goals and agreements and
Challenges
Planned for this lifetime
The heavens were configured just so
And the astrologers say that Pisces is
My sun sign
I am still living this life

In late October of 1997
Using DNA extracted from me
Scientists cobbled an exact copy
All my genes were dominant!

They say the Everly Brothers
Made such wonderful harmony
Because their vocal chords were linked
Genetically
I anticipated making beautiful
Music with my new self
Momentarily forgetting that
I cannot sing very well

We were identical
Junior and I

Or so we thought
But a different alignment
At the moment of cloning
Meant that the Universe
Had a different blueprint in store

The new me died tragically at age 5
In a bathtub electrocution
My grief was somewhat placated
Knowing that the other Juniors
Are only about 50 percent
Copies, while my Junior relished
His 100 percent status

Yes, cloning is amazing science
But it does not compare with
The beauty and grandeur of
Nature's masterwork —

The elephant

THE RECOVERY ROOM

Not the place where your chair is being recovered
Just a small facility performing out-patient surgery –
A Stop'n'Slice
Where the hallway doubled as the recovery room
A good friend was semi-conscious
That hour under anesthesia lost to her forever
Her face alarmingly swollen
After an elective surgery
That 90 percent of her had voted in favor of

I thought of another hospital bed
Where my four-year old lay unrecognizable
A baseball bat having transformed his face
I had to see his left eye but could not

His purple star faded over fifteen years
Transitory traumas once so painful
Finally forgotten
Unlike the finality of a death

I'm querulous –
Whatever happened to the Age of Aquarius?
I held out hope that the twentieth century
Would be the last millennium we refer to as
The Dark Ages
I held out hope

Yet we still kill animals with guns
And worse
We still do war

Today a serial killer pleaded guilty to the murder of 48 young women
He appeared in court in an orange, prison jump-suit, spectacles, manacles,
And a new haircut.
Armed with scissors, what went through the prison barber's mind?
Just another day at the office?
Was he tempted?
Would I have been?

A Certain Smile

Certain sensual smiles
Offered up on occasion
Hinting of bliss in
The perfect extra bend in
The line of the lips' curve
Parting and closing
In anticipation
Eyes agleam with
Unmysterious depths
Past or future pleasures
Little laugh lines
So alive
A silent flash
Steals her face and
Reflects off her eyes
This early evening
Her lips slightly parted
She glides
The two of us
Already joined
In some special union
Years before we touch or
Admit to any attraction
Or even talk comfortably
About anything

Or even meet

It's already understood

And palpable

The sirens' call

That quietly screams

To me of

A great union

Two souls

Craving the completion

Offered in

A certain smile

One Car - Two Drivers

One   **Two**

That bastard cut me off
He will pay dearly

                                                                         What a blessed place
                                                                         I live in
                                                                         And today I'm truly in it

That one can't keep track of who first arrived
At the intersection
What's his Imbecility Quotient?

                                                                         I drive by robot
                                                                         And take in all I can:
                                                                         The lush green canopy of
                                                                         Giant maples and alders
                                                                         The purview of the horizon
                                                                         The purr of this fine machine

That guy behind me is following too closely
Maybe I'll slam on my brakes

                                                                         From the radio leaps
                                                                         Knofler's incandescent guitar
                                                                         Syncopated to my synapses
                                                                         Sweeter than an angel's harp
                                                                         Treasure amongst
                                                                         The push-buttons
                                                                         I am right here

That imbecile on the radio cannot
Complete a sentence
My eyes are on the pavement
I refuse the rest of the world
I am not here

                                        Look, a jogger and her dog
                                        Their hair is the same
                                        Beautiful shade of
                                        Golden red

Look at that jogger
What a body
If there was a God,
She'd be naked

                                        The wonder of seeing
                                        A two-legged and
                                        A four-legged creature
                                        Running in sync

"King of Pain" is on the radio…how can a
Grown man call himself "Sting?"
I wish I had a carton of eggs – I'd open
The sunroof and pummel
The next driver who doesn't respect me

                                        That person is in a big hurry
                                        And I'm in a position to help
                                        Thank goodness

MAYBE ALASKA

Maybe Alaska
Or Tierra del Fuego
I want the fiercest coastline
Not pristine, sandy, boring beaches
I want to hear glaciers calving
I want the immaculate devastation of
Horrendous tides, stupendous waves, Tsunami madness
The west coast of Vancouver Island in February
I want to witness eons of erosion
In my miniscule lifespan

If the fourth movement
Of Beethoven's Ninth Symphony
Is our species' finest ever achievement
I want to hear the fifth movement
And I plead the fifth
And I drank a fifth of single-malt
At the Firth of Forth
And still I go forth
While under constant bombardment,
My fireworks fizzling under
Nature's Roman candle extravaganza
Of Red Giants and White Dwarfs
And the universal dark matter
Where hearts and minds joyously collide

And, in the Earth's bellowing bowels and
Regurgitated force-fields
May the elements constantly clash
Let their borders be distorted
Let air fight fire
Let water drown in flesh
Let paper cut scissors
Let earth exist in a gaseous state
How else can I find
Peace, solace and serenity?

I require the hydrogen blast
Of the planet's ecstatic, cataclysmic waltz
Peer past your absorption field
Look around your microscope, your macro lens,
And your digital future
Climb Mount Perception, adjust your viewfinder
One if by land, two if bi-focal
Direct your attention
Toward that most preposterously tumultuous
Site in all the Universe
Where the cobbling of new life transpires
Where the extraordinary comes into being
Where unimaginable beauty is born
And where I once was a kibitzer

Sleetness and White

As a drizzly day unfolded I
Happened upon a wandering minstrel
And wondered whether we

Could wonder together when
Our eyes locked and our
Smiles snowballed

Sweetly showering us with
Pristine white rose petals
And a temporary tornado

Of dervishness derailed
My unequal librium and
A thunderbolt took hold

Back I had to tell myself
You know another case of
Unrequired love when

You breathe it in and further
More's the pity the poor
Squandering squeal of

Love's bloom and boom
The drizzle turned to sleet but
Something new was illuminated

An Olympic flame
Eternally torching
My enlarged minstrel heart

THE LAST POEM

The last poem I wrote was about this one
And this one is about the next one
I'll be doing what poets do:
Comparing things
In an attempt to convey a meaningful image

One image will be of the laugh of a 4 year old:
I'll write "blowing soap bubbles of joy"
Another will be an old man on a park bench
Adrift in reverie or maybe melancholy
His chin and both hands resting on his cane
I'll write "if only this driftwood could talk"

Would that I could convey
That wonderful feeling I have
Listening to a Bach contata
But to do that sensation justice
I may resort to hyperbole, given the limitations of
Our meager vocabulary, which in no way
Covers the myriad variations of sight and sound
And touch and feel and feelings and emotions
That comprise our worlds, and which lack leaves us
Struggling for simile to express ourselves

By the time the poem after the next one rolls around
Luckily, we will have parsed all the Universe
And expanded our vocabularies accordingly

We will no longer use simile or metaphor
Instead, the poetry prize will be awarded for
Hyper-accurate statements such as
"The sunset measured 9.2 on the International
Standard Beauty Scale, with a red-orange-purple factor
Of seventy-two"

And then all the poets will be able to retire
Some with only 14 and a half minutes of fame
And all poetic licenses and learners' permits
Will be revoked

PALO ALTO AND BEYOND

I.

Palo Alto
Perth Australia
Pulmonary artery
Personal assistant
Pop art
Power amp
Passive aggressive
Problem area
Pennsylvania Avenue
Penny ante
Paying alimony
Panic alarm
Pan Am
Peace accord
Palindromic Anna
Partially ambidextrous
(right hand only)

II.

Alfred Prufrock
Able-bodied person
Apple Powerbook
Airmail package
Ancient Persia
Any port
Amboy Perth
Asian Pacific
Aunt Penny
Austin Powers
Anti-pasti
Animal pelt
Assistance please
Award presentation
Angular profile
Almost perfect
(pi out of four)

FLYING BUTTRESSES

Mom,
Before I go to sleep
Will you please read me
My Miranda rights?
I like the part where
Anything I say
Can be used against me
I always wonder if it
Can also be used *for* me
What about when I affirm life
Or wax poetically
Or wane haltingly
Like we both sometimes do
I so love your reading voice
What about when I
Support the person next to me
Like you taught me to do
I am the gauze on Miranda's wound
I am a flying buttress
If someone wants to use that against me
Bring it on!

Pops,

Can we play catch today?

I don't want to keep score

I don't want you to let me win at chess

I don't want to be taught a lesson

I want to be taught an art

I want to know how to nurture

I want to know what compassion means

I don't want soccer trophies on my shelf

I don't want you to brag about my skill

I want to be freed from negativity

I want my mitt to develop a beautiful sheen

Like the feeling I have

When you toss me the ball

In a rainbow's arc

At the perfect speed

To allow me to succeed

Your subtle succor helps me stretch

And evolve into a

Flying buttress for my teammates

And the cathedral

Myself

I Plan to Abdicate (abridged version)

Someone told me that I should work on my "abs"
I absorbed this suggestion without abnegation and
Recognized that many possibilities abound
Like abeyance and abundance and

Abduction, absurdity and abnormality and
Ablution, abandonment and abusiveness and
Absentia, abrasion and travel abroad
Or turning aboriginal in my humble abode

The challenge abrades and could prove abominable
And I so abhor indecision's abyss and
Now I'm ably abetted by a clear choice…
Abdication, what a lovely concept

Now I don't hold a throne or feel particularly royal
I know nothing of abstaining or abrogating
And I have never absolved anyone nor
Abjured any doctrine, so how do I qualify?

I know that King Edward the VIIIth abdicated
So that he could marry an American
Something I have done twice
So there is that in my favor

Any abdication undertaken by me
Will rightly observe all circumstantial pomp
And I swear to abide faithfully and
With the utmost honor and enthusiasm

I'll put my left hand on a bibliography
And raise my right hand high and give
You my solemn vow that my abdication
Will be one of historical significance

And I promise to abolish anything that impedes
Our search for the answers

LUTHER BEURRE BLANC PARK

Early, early dawn down water's edge
Sunrise silver silent lake
A week's worth of wildflowers undisturbed by
Power mowers and weed whackers
Which won't arrive till 7:00 A.M.
A Chocolate Food Retriever
Celebrates, singing
"My life is brilliant"
To himself, sniffing the light fantastic
Bowl-filled dreams
Ahh, if only these odors could talk
To my muscle-bound beauty
Perhaps they must do
In some eloquent way
For he cannot get enough

Nights Like This

Mama said there'd be nights like this:
My smoothie had lumps
My chewing gum had gingivitis
Rogaine did nothing for my bald tires
My deviled Egg-Beaters were a total failure
My hybrid car is half-giraffe
A Sloppy-Joe sandwich, sure enough, ruined my shirt
Despite the q-tips I missed my cue
An awl did not make me holy
My "Act of Contrition" was just an act
My knap sack was full of siesta
The Harry Potter movies were not in claymation
There were no instructions with my new comb
And

I sat for a very long time
At a railroad crossing
Watching a freight rumble pass:
Hoppers, box cars, gondolas, containers, tankers –
A satisfying display of muscle
And graffiti.
Not counting cars,
Just content and expectant
Awaiting the payoff
But denied!

No caboose....

Ah, well
Spring hopes eternally --
My warped vinyl records sound great at warp speed, and
I do take comfort in knowing Diana Ross is the Supreme being
I feel as indispensable as a broken gumball machine
And I remain faithlessly yours,
For I am
Richard the cowardly-lion-hearted

UPHILL BATTLE

Was it
"The Taming of the Shrew?"
Or "The Turn of the Screw?"
Driver orange juice
OJ chase Manhattan sky line
Up the ante chips
Wins the pot head
For the hills from which
The water falls
Surely to the sea
Cruise the bars
Wine and dine with
Thyme waits for no one is missed
Amidst the
Garden of earthly delights
The eye as well as the
Palate it be, whisper words of
Welcome to the organic farm-
Aid, AIDS, E-bola, botulism
Food poisoning
Legionnaire's disease
At ease, troops mess-hall
KP duty where
Blasphemous poetry
Par-boils on the back burner
A simmering risotto up front

And center yourself for

You are what you leap over

All the Everests

Standing between you

And your perfect

You

The University of Humanity

First there was the word
Has it that Gabriel blew his horns
Of a dilemma Bovary whose ovaries
From minus one to positive thinking
About the nature of the universal
Laws governing mankind's evolution
This materialistic like glue, keep
Your nose to the grindstoned
Out of your mindlessness
Approaching the doors of perception, and
While at the doorway you ask yourself,
Isadora Duncan? No,
But a Yo-Yo is, and
Yo-Yo Ma plays cello,
And Yo Ma-Ma done told you that
You're the exception that proves the rule
That was spared to spoil the child
That is the father to the man
And the women of wisdom,
Greater than knowledge of
The all too brief history of time by Hawking
His wares and wherefore art thou
Shalt not use thy words in vain
In vanity, all is vanity or is it
The way you say hello in spring
And goodbye in the winter of our discontents

Listed on the side of the carton

Of cigarettes and cocktails off

We go, into the wild blue yonderlust

For the truth

Which sets you free

Free at last,

Great God Almighty, it's a gas, gas, gasoline

Is the real reason for the call to arms

Missing from the statue of Venus

Circling the Sun on Spaceship Earth

Bound for glory and going for the gold and the silver

Lining the walls of the halls of Montezuma and

The shores of trampoline mean peace machine

In a parallel universes don't frighten me

It's the perpendicular ones you have to watch out – we've been hit!

We humpty off the wall and

Roll off a logarithm of

Four beats to the bar

Code stamped on the ID tag

You're it! – our first graduate

Of the University of Humanity

Summa cum laude laude laude

Laudable new curriculum --

Countries without borders

Politics without testosterone

Religion without symbols
Holistic inspiration and
Wordless poetry

The Astronauts

Charles Darwin passed on
Before the evolution of
The three-olive martini
He missed out entirely on
Telemarketing, super-spreader events, and
The deification of falsehood
He died before
The species had evolved sufficiently
To come to terms with mortality
Or cure it

Like passed stones
Opportunities blown
From dust unto dust bin
Everything transmutes
My cells will decompose and
End up somewhere nurturing something

Little consolation, though
Lives of thirst and hunger
For the resolution of
Consciousness and mortality

Consciousness is Nature's
Finest achievement
But ultimately just a tease
As death cheats us of it

Seven astronauts perished
Seconds after take-off
When the Challenger exploded
And that latter group
On the Columbia
Died upon re-entry
We consoled ourselves saying:
"They died doing what they love"
Conveniently overlooking the fact that
What they really loved to do was
Live

Unrequired Love

When first you said
We must have known each other in another life
I thought it was the future
My favorite tense

Though our lives had intertwined
Purely randomly
A greater force had ensured
That our souls' vectors would intersect
At that exact second

Vectors interact
According to the soul's blueprint
For a life's possibilities
Offering all potential heart-links
Oblivious to all other karmic debt
And responsibilities
Sometimes in perfect synchronicity
Other times when grander purposes
Must be served
And love is bold
But must be put on hold

When your tongue slid from my mouth
And you quickly breathed
"I gotta get out of here"

Or maybe it was
"I can't do this"
I knew exactly
What you meant

BREAKING WAVES

Self-propelled phrases
Eject from a
Spiral bound mind
Nightwatch glistened and
The morning Sun shone on
Bare fruit trees
Coming to fruition while
The bifurcated brain struggling for unity
Seeking solace at the seashore
And inspiration in the breaking waves

But the revelation was that I
Was the one that was broken
And that any salvation would be
My becoming the wave,
Defiant, resolute, fierce,
And eternal.

My God

Scribbling my unruly verse
Between the ruled lines of
An illegal pad
In an attempt to capture
However fleetingly
The feeling

And record it for posterity
In regal perpetuity
But lacking a thesaurus and
Searching the Encyclopedia through
Volume "TUV"
I scramble for the right words

I read the New English Dictionary from
"Aardvark" to "Zzardvark"
Every volume of Shakespeare
Everything I could get my brain on

I majored in English
And minored in English
As a second language
I joined a writers' workshop
Sought to amuse a muse

I paid the piper and
Paid my dues
And everything I've checked out
Is overdue and

It's driving me sane
The two great hemispheres of
Language and memory extant
In extremely gray matter

It's right there for the taking
It's on the tip of my third tongue
It's looming, imminent,
Coming into view

Why it's
It's
It's
My god,
It's you
And
I

THE PATHETIC OCEAN

Mood swings
Through arcs
Of triumph
Over small things,
Life's little miseries
Miniseries of roots and
Trunks and hope chests
Heave and breathe a
Suffocating toxic noxious
Nausea, No Exit nor
Endgame playing possum
Winsome, want some
Major successes

But the air is thick with
The souls of those
Who vanished into thin air

More's the
Pity, petty, pathetic tac toe
The line up for the
Peace Train, hard rain, ball and chain of
Fools rush in where
Depression soon follows the
Leader down the rabbit hole
For four square and
Seven years ago a ghost

Appeared as an a cappella
Speaker in surround sound track to
A holographic film coating the
Lens of the periscope
Peering out of the pathetic ocean
Espying the land of transformation
On the impossibly distant shore

LOST AND FOUND

On the nightly news they
Reported on the number of
Unfortunate ones
Who had lost their lives

I wondered if mine was
Lost as well and if so
Was it completely
And irretrievably thus

There are so many blank
Spots gone forever
Dark, drunk, discordant
Stretches of gloom

The wasted years of school
Two decades of organized
Religion and another
Thirty spent in some

Middle management mindset
Witnessing good people go glum
Brandishing false power
And living in fear and the

Blind pursuit of instinctual
Desires without self-awareness
The mind justifying any old
Impulse from the brain

But I am not so saddened that
I can't keep moving forward
For I still feel fortunate in
Knowing there's much left to be found

FAR ENOUGH

Just one look took

My breath away but

Luckily not too far

Because I needed it back to

Whisper sweet nothings

In her ear and

She asked me if nothing

Can have any quality at all

Let alone sweetness

And I said

"Brilliant insight"

And she said

"You heard it here first"

And I said

"No, I heard it here"

Pointing to my ears

And she said

"If you want to get technical"

And I said

"Yes oh yes, please yes"

And she laughed and said

"Great minds think alike"

And I said

"Great minds don't resort to clichés; besides

It's their uniqueness that makes them great"

And she said

"Alright, Buster"

And I said

"Did you really say 'buster'?"

And she said

"You seemed so non-chalant"

And I said

"I'm very chalant"

And she said

"Oh, yeah, now that you mention it,

It's written all over you"

So I quickly exfoliated

And she called me a flake

So I said

"Sticks and stones"

And she said

"Which is your preference?"

To which I reminded her that

"Gentlemen prefer blonds"

And she said

"Gentle is good but I like it a little rough"

And I said

"I love you from the bottom of my heart"

And she said

"Which ventricle?"

And she added

"And what about the center,
Your heart of hearts?"
And I said
"Did you study anatomy?"
And she said
"Only that of four different men"
And I said
"All men are different"
And she said
"I dated identical twins"
"Who are they?" I queried
And she said
"They shall remain nameless"
And I said
"They don't have names –
Doesn't that compound the confusion?"
And she said
"Talk about confusing!"
And I said
"Great minds don't get confused"
And she said
"I think they do"
And I said
"Do they even think at all?"
And she said
"They think of All"

And I said

"It's all or nothing with you"

And she said

"It's all or nothing whether I'm

Involved or not"

And I said

"Are you involved?"

And she said

"Involving is closer to the truth"

And I said

"Your beauty is my truth"

And it takes my breath away

But not too far

MARY

Hail Mary
My lovely friend
Some day
You and I are
Going to have to
Go out
Behind the barn
And do something
Intellectual

Returnity

When an overcast sky collapses
And individual clouds are born
Light exposes their many facets
Character and colors
All heaven breaks loose

You may not know the day
Your cord of destiny
Starts to unwind or
Suddenly snaps
And you're gone
Like a cloud

In constant motion
Transmuting, evolving
At times a perfect shape
At other times blobular
Once, isolated and
Traveling to the beat of a
Different drum major
Other times bouncing off
Your brethren

You inspire and
You generate joy
You're awesome
Mistaken for fog

Hidden by mist
You cling to mountaintops in fear
You can get gloomy
Rain on parades and
Spoil picnics at will

But you nurture
You cause life
You dissipate and reform
You peter out
And in
Tossed turbulently
Sailing serenely
One moment you resemble a
Turnip, the next a
Wild yucca

You appear and disappear
And reappear in
Continual transformation
Until the day your ship comes out
And the sky turns black
And I turn blue

Until you return

Take Care

What happens here, stays there
That wasn't then, this isn't now
Then two in the hand
Me downs, discards, tattered, torn, mutilated
Some time I'll be a first born
To be wild
Freedom's just another word for
Nothing left to climb
One's way up mount syphilis
The unending quest
Toward enlightenment at
The hands of some master
Of fact totem pole position
Yourself for the slalom gates
Open to Nirvana and remember
Your needy, hungry, homeless cohorts
Who inhabit the dark reaches of the
Underworld where you stick your proboscis
And discover that
Just as one should take care
One must also give it

The Map of the United States

There are three Davenports in the United States and two in my parlor

There are 37 Columbias, but none in the District of Columbia

A small village with many laundromats, Washington, lent its name to both a

State and the nation's capital – how confusing

Did the framers of the Constitution do this?

I ask because many of the states have beveled edges.

Most of them are at least partially delineated by a river or some natural border

But not even the Great Divide swayed those linear thinkers who gave us the rectangles

Known as Colorado and Wyoming

On the map, one day, there appeared a great Crop Circle,

Exactly four-hundred miles across,

Centered in Dodge City

Where cattle had fertilized the ground an eternal black

Everything within the circle's circumference was obliterated:

People, cattle, farms, golf tees, theater marquees, grange halls,

Prairie mice, mouse pads, churches, schools, Barbie-doll collections,

Power plants, prisons, kaleidoscopes, hospitals, and Tarot-card decks –

All gone

The only things left were the 212 planes and boats

That had disappeared in the Bermuda Triangle between 1800 and 1960

Somehow transported to the circle

CNN said it was another hoax, this time gone terribly awry

The President said it was an act of terror

The Prime Minister offered his support and sympathy

The thoughts and prayers of the King of Sweden were with us

Or so he said 'cause that's what you say

On her school room map of the Western Hemisphere

A young girl in Tehran stuck her compass point into Dodge City

And circumscribed the circle

Then, she cut the circle out of the map

Across the world, normal activity halted

Commerce was in chaos except for the merchandising of

Guns and lanterns and water and gas masks and crop-circle-dusting
     planes

And a freeze-dried dream or two

The Pope offered a feeble wave, attributing the disaster to the hand of
     the devil

A Hollywood script-writer set to work

Real estate developers started frothing, while

Priests and looters salivated

Two co-workers in Tallahassee hurriedly rented a motel room

The armed forces mobilized, and Mobile came out in force

The aliens, who had no trouble at all identifying their flying object

Were giving each other high-eights and cackling insidiously

But there is no need to panic

Faith springs eternal

There's still a place on the map

Somewhere North of the Black Hole

Where Custer made his next-to-last stand

Where the map is the territory

And GPS cannot find us

We will be there soon

The Weather Report

The weatherperson on the 6:00 news

Is telling me that it's 50 in Puyallup

And 51 degrees in Black Diamond

And 49 in Ports Townsend and Orchard

A high of 48 in Friday Harbor

Fifty-two degrees in Bellingham, Bremerton, Burlington,

And Bainbridge Island

These minute differences are repeated

Night after night

Someone cares I suppose

But I'd rather know

Is there bliss in Bellevue?

How's the mood in Maple Valley?

And, while we're at it

How are the folks in Fauntleroy feeling tonight?

Did anyone in Langley find a silver dollar today

While combing the beach?

I would be fascinated to hear which city

My lost memories now reside in

Whether my soul's essence twin

Happens to live in North Bend

That the meaning of life is

Buried in the hills around Issaquah

And

Are the stars at night

Big and bright

Deep in the heart?

Pandemic II

I thought it would come from underground
Troop transport tread marks inbound
But there was no human element to
The scourge

Images of a green ball of nerf
Wreaking havoc all 'round the Earth
Pink cocktail umbrellas protruding from
The scourge

In my wildest dreams I never dreamt
It would cause such carnage, who sent
Us such a destructive weapon
The scourge

At first though, we started out strong
It didn't seem like it would last too long
Perhaps we'd make it through this together
The scourge

We could handle it if we were bold
Spend some time with the world on hold
A hiccup in time at worst
The scourge

But soon the death toll took its toll
Masks appeared on many smart souls
While hellos and waves grew tentative
The scourge

We knew the politicians would feed us lies
But trusted the doctors to be wise
Most of us did as we were told during
The scourge

Omnipresent grey clouds loomed above
Psychological damage there was plenty of
Isolation is the grim reality of
The scourge

A sense of doom like a ball of fire
Overdue phone calls came over the wire
Attempts to resolve old shit before disaster hit
The scourge

And there was a concomitant, magnetic hand
Beckoning us to succumb to the death knell and
Bow to the unholy allure of
The scourge

Statistics can work at a subconscious level
The rising numbers were like the devil
Fight them off you must
The scourge

Should I strive to overcome, to squelch my fear
Slay the dragon, to seize the year
Could I muster a fight against
The scourge?

Quicksand beckoning the unready
A whirlpool, a vortex, a depression eddy
To where, sadly, souls are swallowed up by
The scourge

Do better, best I heard in a dream
Silly me, I hummed a Rocky theme
There had to be a way to conquer
The scourge

But when what I wanted was to explode
All I could muster was a toehold
The red smudge of courage was all I earned
The scourge

Racism raised its insidious head
Rampant ignorance was blatantly fed
So many innocents lost their lives
The scourge

Now it's a year since I did deliver
To the firemen their carbs and sugar
But monthly donuts wouldn't have helped them with
The scourge

Reopening restaurants was a hot topic
Compliance with safety measures became myopic
Regression to the mean was taking hold
The scourge

And now another, another week arrives
I've lost another year of the Grandkids' lives
Perhaps I have learned a thing or three from
The scourge

On reflection, my reflective skills have been honed
The wisdom of silence – loud as a trombone
I have made it part-way through
The scourge

But there is not another side
Just the ebb and flow of our species ride
Conforming to deviations and ultimately subsuming
The scourge

We have made one small step for mankind
And another one for man-not-so-kind
We have witnessed bravery and ugliness too
The scourge

Join in with me if you would
Let us become a force for good
Our lives need not be ever defined by
The scourge

THE WHY CHROMOSOME

The centers of her perfectly circumscribed buttocks
Are less than the diameter of either apart –
Thus the globes intersect, competing for space
Gracefully, non-tangentially

This, I gather, upon the most rudimentary of inspections
Through turquoise gym shorts
Heaven forfend the day they are removed
Revealing perfectly tattooed renderings of
The Earth's western and eastern hemispheres
Crying out for some global warming

Men are castigated, at times
For their adoration of the female form
Yet they find beauty everywhere

I am transfixed by a flock of starlings
More miraculous in their movements
Than the Blue Angels.
Myriad shapes
The starling flock in flux
As its members spiral and loop and dart
Often maniacally yet in
A synchronized unity
Tuned into some power wave
My receptors aren't

And my lover's skin: every square centimeter

Following in lockstep, each in place, smooth, intact,

Defining contiguous

Perfectly inter-connected

Flesh flies freely

Regardless of the gyrations her body puts it through

Unending new shapes as she

Simply rolls over

In our aerie

San Francisco and Beyond

I.	II.
San Francisco	Fast start
Santa Fe	Fire starter
Seventy-five	Forty-six
Sexy freaks	Four score
Set free	Far shore
Silly fool	Full stomach
Sinn Fein	Feeling slow
Sally Fields	Fail safe
Sang-froid	Free sex
South Fork	Frank Sinatra
So far	Feng shui
Strictly friends	Fifty-seven
When I'm	Why, I'm a
Sixty-four	Free spirit

Mutiny on Nature's Bounty

Dion sang, "Here's my story, it's sad but true"
Nostradamus predicted his predictions would result in a
Best seller
Chicken Little and Galileo
Conducted experiments with gravity
Johnny Horton sang, "Please, Mr. Custer, I don't wanna go!"
Malthus foresaw us running out of mojo
The Who claimed we wouldn't be fooled again
Huxley concluded the human experiment could fail

Neanderthals graffiti-over their cave-paintings while
Bipeds on tandem bicycles circle endlessly and
Cockneys start pronouncing "H" alf-eartedly
The Great Wall of China, upon further consideration, is deemed to be just so-so
The Berlin Wall is resurrected
Micro-organisms stage a sit-in
Jeremiah denies he was ever a bullfrog
A woman who had been cremated turns over in her urn
Bacteria declare a righteous cause
Deviant microbes act out their wicked fantasies
Christo encircles the Mount Rushmore monument with a billion barnacles
Mad cows enroll in an anger management class
Five intellectual maggots hold a bed-in like John and Yoko
Rabbit ear antennae and lucky rabbit feet are put in a time capsule
Then forever forgotten
Viruses attend an ad-hoc rally at La Place Pigalle

Protons and neutrons don't care what's in store
A lifetime achievement award is given to a four-year old
The siamang's shrill screech horrifies
Ebonics replaces Esperanto as the universal hope
Schizophrenia becomes airborne
And a Dungeness crab holds up a victory claw

As seagulls squabble over an Oreo ort
And cormorants dance derisively on the bow
A rogue wave tumbles a toddler into a mischievous surf, and
Some endangered species laughs its last few laughs
Not realizing that he who laughs last
Is horribly alone

TWO YOUNG MEN GIVING DIRECTIONS

After a dinner of enchiladas with their stepmother
Two young men give her directions to the freeway
Yearning to shine in her love
The competitive fire burns as they
Posit contradictory routes

A rivalry of spatial reasoning
The brandishing of superior knowledge
Both so very smart
But confusing knowledge with integrity
It's a duel to the start

She smiles acceptance and encouragement
And sees their final bouts of boyhood
Their lives unfurling in
A quiet quibble before
Turning in for the flight

As the three drive off
In their own directions
A triangle of love membrane
Grows and covers
An ever-widening area

Creating a net to provide safe landing

Should succor be required

And a catapult to jettison them

Into the stratospheric first step

On their sacred journeys

Tombstone Territory

It wasn't the best of times
It wasn't the worst of times
It did provide a framework though
Mankind was still seriously lost

The horror of the Korean war
The paranoia of the cold war
The insanity of Viet Nam
The waste of the oil wars

I received sustenance from
Many wonderful artists and
I got to witness some
Important advances

But greed and deceit were rampant and
People still hunted for sport and there
Was that fool who sang to himself
"Imagine no John Lennon"

Next time around I would like to be
Left-handed, able to whistle through
My fingers and basically be
A lean keen loving machine

We still believe our thoughts to be true

So it was, so it goes, so it's gone

Ashes to ashes, dust off my tombstone

And check the hyper-links to other important gravesites

Etched below my name

BREASTS

Sometime during her
Fifty-first year
Her breasts laid down
For a well-needed rest
And
Finding a certain serenity
In the reposed position
Decided they would stay there
For the rest of her
Remaining, vibrant
Thirty-five years

George Bernard Saw

If I could see what
George Bernard saw
I'd see
A huge foam "We're Number 1" finger on top
Of the Statue of Liberty
Tears leaking from a Buddha statue
A vegan drinking a Beefeaters, and
A feather Boa Constrictor

I am standing on a corner
Handing out PF Flyers
You see
And wishing Albert Camus
Had been wearing a seat belt
And JFK rode the popemobile
And I await the next bottom feeding
Scheduled for just about now

Alas, my empty trophy case is
A shadow of its future self
I want to see
I am not superstitious
But I definitely am stitious
I. M. Pei'd up
And there's a narrow load ahead
I know we'll squeeze through

There's an awful lot of Lenya

Where that came from

See

It's just grim, my brother

This gruesome situation

It's as tacky as a bulletin board

No, it's as tacky as an

Equestrian supply store

And maybe like a whale's tail

I could be a fluke of nature

I can't see

Where it's all headed

And I think I'm being tailed

For Lent I'm giving up

I'll always strive to be myself

Even if I can't

Dark Crow

Were I a better birder I'd know
The difference between a raven and a crow
Bi-polar or manic-depressive
Fine distinctions addle me so

It's darkness that confuses me
Blindness is my plight
So I ask you now may I
Return into your glorious light?

The distant rainbow's color spectrum ranges
From white to gray to black
Your wondrous firecracker heart
Would take a safecracker to crack

You're as wild as a conflagration
A nightmare's tattooed on your back
I won't try an intervention or
Smoke your mentholated crack

But there is one thing I'd ask of you
Were light the predominant fact
Is there any room in your wild, rambunctious heart
Where you'd deign to take me back?

Years Together

When we were much younger
Spring was upon us
The lust was consummate, unflagging
All our thoughts were about
The last time
Or the next time
All imagery devoted to
Our bodies together
A ceaseless exploration of
Give and take
And push and pull
And cause and effect

Toward the middle
When flesh started its descent
And desire dropped
In a concomitant swoon
We expanded the imagery
For a carnal boost
And laughed about new kinds of joy
And intimacy
And talked about love
Versus being in love

Then came the years of total capitulation
Earth and gravity reclaiming what was theirs

Where once was a stately construct
A lost longing lay languid
Where once reigned regal globes
Of youthful beauty
Worldliness swung

And speaking of swinging
Now that I'm past it
How about putting me
Out to stud?

WATER BORDERS

One day the Oceans and Seas got organized and
Declared their separate sovereign identities:
The Antarctic States, the Republic of the North Atlantic
The United Soviet State of South Pacific Water Molecules and Fish
And so on

With their independent status
They created boundaries and governments
And waged wars and emulated the land nations
In most aspects
Save disease and famine
The United Oceans implemented the
Universal Water Species Food Chain Code

A great wall was erected between those bodies formerly known as
The Gulf of Mexico and the Atlantic Ocean
Disastrously disrupting
The Gulf Stream and global climate patterns
This resulted in the extinction of 218 already iffy species

One day an unintentionally rogue Orca
Crossed from the North to the South Atlantic
Without shots, a passport, or a visa
A team of sonar-controlled, high-speed, border-patrol jelly fish
Swooped in, in response to the alarm,
Forcing the frightened, lonely mammal to an ocean-floor holding tank

From where it could not surface for air

And subsequently, sadly, died

Leading to the establishment of Amnesty InterOceania

Each ocean designed its own flag in celebration of its independence

They all had a sea-blue field

With various versions of

A white wave motif to distinguish them

When the aquatic mammals and fish

Encountered each other's flags

And realized they were all swimming swimmingly

They recognized their common fishmanity,

Tore down the wall

Blew the boundaries out of the water

Swore off the emulation of man

And once again were able to

Patrol the planet in peace

And to love unconditionally

CHOOSING A CHRISTMAS CARD IN 2005

There's a funny one with an elf's feet,
One with a beautiful rendering of a white fir
Against a blue-black sky
And the one with the dove
Could be appropriate

But nothing feels quite right
After reading another 37 were killed in Iraq today
Can any image convey
What I feel?

Perhaps I should follow the lead of
The Beatles' White Album
And keep it simple
And appropriately, outwardly silent

And inside, the right words
To offer a sense of hope
Maybe I'll encourage a more generous use of
"Bless you!"

Or, given the war and the worry
That many members of the human species
Are devolving,
I'll settle on these words:

"May your next glorious incarnation
On this wondrous planet
Occur in an era of
Peace and harmony"

And I'm drifting along
In a tumbling tumble-dream

GRACELAND

In the blink of an eye
Of the needle in a
Haystack stuck in a
Rut eternally damned
Over the spillway
Into the maelstrom
The female storm
The barricades to
Realization and fulfillment of
Life's larger purpose
The "Higher Love"
The greater good
Gracious me
"Can't we all just get along?"
Long way to tip a waiter
Water food shelter me
Cover me
Surround me with love
Before I
Ascend to heaven's gate
Can't wait for
Transcendental souls to
Matriculate
To a solid state of
Grace

CATHOLISCHISM

I've been recovering furniture for several years and a
Recovering catholic for fifty-seven and I believe in
Forgiveness whole-heartedly and I'm big on hope
And charity but I have little faith in organized religion
However, I do love the church for making me

Financially independent when they settled out of court for
Fifteen million after I sued for gross and serious abuse for
Making me feel my pubescent sexuality was
Gross and serious abuse while the
Graft and lies and abuse run rampant and

They continue to encourage the meek to even more meekness
By turning over their destiny to a higher power when every
Higher power I've ever conversed with recommended
Listening to the higher-self for one's guiding light
Perhaps someday they'll start to really analyze the bible and

Recognize that women are human beings and maybe
I'll decide to rejoin if the rumors are true and the 83rd
Vatican Council decides to simplify and condense the commandments
Such that one of the new ones reads:
"Thou Shalt Not Covet Thy Neighbor's Wife in Vain"

Too Smart

It's not too smart
To be too smart
For your own good

And it's not too dumb
To be too smart
For your own bad

But it is too smart
To be too smart
For your own bad

And it is too dumb
To be too smart
For your own good.

STARRY NIGHT

It was a STARRY NIGHT when
The NIGHT WATCH caught
THE HUNTERS IN THE SNOW
Stopping at a CAFE TERRACE AT NIGHT where
THE NIGHTHAWKS were having their
LAST SUPPER and discussing
THE THREE AGES OF WOMEN —
THE BIRTH OF VENUS,
The NUDE SITTING ON A DIVAN, and
The TAHITIAN WOMEN

The following day, MONA LISA and
THE GIRL WITH THE PEARL EARRING
Immersed in the IRISES, and
THE WHEATFIELDS WITH CYPRESSES
And all of PRIMAVERA, like
A SUNDAY AFTERNOON ON THE ISLAND OF LA
       GRANDE JATTE with
The WATER LILIES and the
LUNCHEON OF THE BOATING PARTY, and
THE BATHERS, and of course
THE KISS

And after THE DANCING CLASS at
THE SCHOOL OF ATHENS
They juggled CAMPBELL'S SOUP CANS

And in their joy let out THE SCREAM heard by
WHISTLER'S MOTHER who, inspired by her
SELF-PORTRAIT WITH THORN NECKLACE
Fought THE GREAT WAR ON FACADES
Opening to a COWS SKULL WITH CALICO ROSES and
DOGS PLAYING POKER — indelible images all . . .
Due to THE PERSISTENCE OF MEMORY

A Mind of Gold

What's that?
Oh, I'm awake
The dream is just disappearing
The world was going to end just a few seconds ago
Now I cannot remember why

After spooning my partner more tightly than
Minnesota cuddles Wisconsin
I get untangled but
Remain tangled up in
"Tangled Up In Blue"
A more current musical landing place than
Where I had alit twenty-four hours earlier:
The oboe part of "Peter and the Wolf"

To the bathroom for some
Non-ethnic cleansing
Feeling luckier than the rabbit
Who surrendered her foot
To grace my keychain,
I prioritize my day

My goal is to find a mind of gold.
This will take planning
I cannot be an unguided missile
A sense of purpose
Is required

I am lively serious
It may be hard to see, but
Deep inside –
Well, a couple inches anyway
I know it is true

Feeling full of kilter
I purchase a mouse pad
With a Ouija Board imprinted on it
And decide to receive the message it provides
By recording where the mouse stops
During my morning web surfing

As usual
I had ordered for some attention deficit
And I surfed like a leaf on the e-wind
Checking Email, following links, being reminded of something
Wondering whatever happened to that dreamgirl
From the fifth grade
My mind completely adrift

After a mere twelve clicks
I looked to see if the Ouija Mouse Pad had
Revealed a message –
It told me
In some uncertain terms
"You are asleep"

BALLOONS AT NIGHT

From a cavalcade of somersaulting silhouettes
An alchemist plucked you and behold:
Bubble-bath beauty
I once held you
In the crook of my right arm
Which I would now forfeit
To ensure your joy
I protect you and grin at
Your burst of Crayola laughter, your
Clumber Spaniel sidekick and
The Cumberland Gap between your teeth loose
Fitting clothes slack off your
Incomplete Kewpie form
I'll buy you a piano and a parasol and para-sailing lessons
Teach you the jitterbug
And "Don't be a litterbug!"
And stroke your hair fair and light
Breezes from the Northern reaches
Your full height
You are all that is right – like a sprig
Of soft-blue on a Cape Plumbago
"Baby, Please Don't Go"
Away anchors aweigh a weight on my
Shoulders no burden so light
Like a leaf or a stick-pin

Corsage aroma junior prom
Memory fading
You're off!

Just past midnight, a spray of balloons
Dance unseen
It takes two to tango
And a line to conga
And at your wedding
I danced alone
For you are the daughter
I never had

About the Author

I am a proud grandfather of three. I live on Mercer Island in the southern portion of Lake Washington. Volunteer jobs, in the Alzheimer's community, occupy much of my time these days. Past proclivities include: computer programming and management, Crisis Volunteer on a Suicide Hotline, custom residential architectural CAD drafting, *New York Times* crossword puzzle construction, and writing.

I have lived the inverse relationship between wages and work fulfillment. The more work, usually on a volunteer basis, to help others, the more personal fulfillment. As I enter my 920th month, with the world in turmoil, I strive to be guided by these words from one of the poems, "worship one another".

CPSIA information can be obtained
at www.ICGtesting.com
Printed in the USA
BVHW070131040921
615741BV00003B/19